CHECKLIST FOR THE BUYER
OF A HOUSE
IN THE UK

SIMON I. DON

Table of contents:

To begin, when considering buying a house, apartment, or family home as a 'first-time' property buyer in the UK, it is important to consider the following checklist:

1. Credit score: If you intend to go the mortgage route; lenders will check your credit score and financial history to assess your creditworthiness.
2. Voters List: Why it is important to be on the UK voters list to buy a property and get a mortgage?
3. Income and employment: Lenders will want to see evidence of your income, employment, and any other sources of income you may have.
4. Deposit: The larger the deposit you can provide, the better your chances of getting approved for a mortgage and at lower interest rates.
5. How can parents assist first time buyers?
6. Bank mortgage brokers.
7. Affordability: Lenders will assess your affordability by looking at your income, outgoings, and other financial commitments to ensure you can afford the mortgage repayments.

8. Types of mortgages: There are different types of mortgages available, such as fixed rate, tracker, and variable rate, and you should research and compare these to find the best option for you. The best place to start is to speak with your bank.

9. Fees: There may be fees associated with taking out a mortgage, such as arrangement fees and valuation fees, which you should consider.

Table of contents:

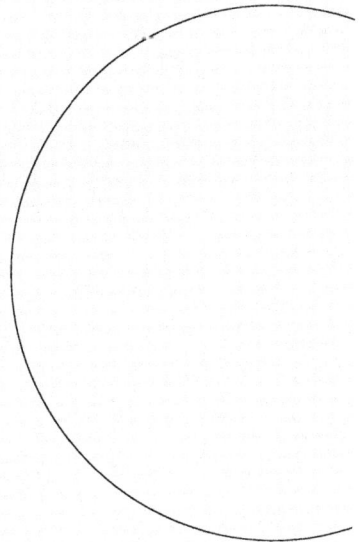

Intro duction.

The benefits of owning a property in the UK include the potential for appreciation: Property prices in the UK have historically risen over time, providing a potential for appreciation. This can be a good investment opportunity, especially in areas with strong economic growth.

Building equity: As a first-time buyer, owning a property can help you to build equity over time, which can be a good investment opportunity.

Conscious saving and planning: Owning a property can also help you to save money each month by compelling you to pay for mortgage payments and other expenses associated with homeownership.

Sense of fulfilment, stability and accomplishment: Buying your first property can provide a sense of accomplishment and stability, as well as a sense of pride in owning your own home.

Rental income: Owning a property can also provide rental income if you choose, eventually, to rent it out.

Overall, owning property in the UK can be a good investment opportunity, but it also comes with its own set of risks and additional responsibilities.

It is important to do your research and carefully consider the pros and cons before making a decision to buy a property.

Additional considerations when buying a property will include:

1. Maintenance and repairs: Owning a property comes with the responsibility of maintaining and repairing it, which can be costly.
2. Risk of negative equity: Property prices can also fall, which can lead to negative equity, meaning that the value of the property is less than the outstanding mortgage.
3. Lack of liquidity: Although a good investment, buying a property ties up a large amount of money and reduces your liquidity, making it harder to respond to unexpected situations.
4. Difficulty in selling: Depending on the market conditions, it can be difficult to sell a property, and it can take a long time to find a buyer.
5. Risk of being a landlord: If you choose to rent out your property, there are risks associated with being a landlord, such as dealing with tenants, rent arrears, legislation and eviction.
6. Legal and regulatory issues: There are also legal and regulatory issues to consider when owning a property, such as laws governing property ownership, property taxes, and other obligations.

CHAPTER N.1

Your credit score.

*

Your credit score.

CREDIT SCORE: LENDERS WILL CHECK YOUR CREDIT SCORE AND FINANCIAL HISTORY TO ASSESS YOUR CREDITWORTHINESS.

The five main phases of buying your property include: **Phase 1.** Checking your credit score. **Phase 2.** Searching for a House; **Phase 3.** Getting a Mortgage; **Phase 4.** Exchange of Contracts; **Phase 5.** Completing the Sale. [Although for efficiency Phase 2 & 3 can be done simultaneously, and it is usually good practice to do this.]

When applying for a mortgage as a first-time property buyer in the UK, one of the most important things to consider is your credit score. Your credit score is a numerical rating that lenders use to assess your creditworthiness and determine whether or not to approve your mortgage application.

Your credit score is based on your credit history, which includes information about your past borrowing and repayment habits. It takes into account factors such as your payment history, credit usage, and the length of your credit history. The higher your credit score, the better your chances of getting approved for a mortgage and at a lower interest rate.

To check your credit score, you can use one of several credit reference agencies in the UK, such as your Bank, Experian, Equifax, or TransUnion. It's a good idea to check your credit score well in advance of applying for a mortgage so that you have time to address any issues that may be negatively impacting your score.

If your credit score is low, it doesn't necessarily mean you won't be able to get a mortgage, but it could make the process more difficult. Lenders may require a larger deposit, or offer a higher interest rate. To improve your credit score, you can take steps such as paying off outstanding debts, correcting any errors on your credit report, and reducing your credit utilization.

It's also important to be aware that when you apply for a mortgage, the lender will carry out a credit check, which will leave a footprint on your credit report. It's important to try and avoid applying for multiple mortgages with different lenders as this can make your credit score worse.

In summary, your credit score is an important factor in getting approved for a mortgage and it's essential to check your credit score well in advance and take steps to improve it if necessary. By being aware of your credit score, you can take the necessary steps to increase your chances of getting approved and at a lower interest rate.

CHAPTER N.2

Voters List: Why it is important to be on the UK voters list to buy a property and get a mortgage?

✳

Voters List:

VOTERS LIST: WHY IT IS IMPORTANT TO BE ON THE UK VOTERS LIST TO BUY A PROPERTY AND GET A MORTGAGE?

Being on the UK voter's list is important when buying a property and getting a mortgage because it can affect your credit score. The voter's list is used by credit reference agencies to verify your identity and to ensure that you are who you say you are. This information is used to create a credit report, which is used by lenders to determine your creditworthiness when you apply for a mortgage.

A credit report is a record of your credit history and includes information such as your current and past addresses, credit accounts, and credit history. Lenders use this information to assess the risk of lending you money and to determine the interest rate and terms of your mortgage. If you are not on the voter's list, it may be more difficult for lenders to verify your history and identity, which can make it harder for you to get a mortgage.

Additionally, being on the voter's list can also affect your ability to vote, as it is a requirement to be on it to be able to vote in the general elections.

It's important to note that being on the voter's list is not the only factor that lenders consider when assessing your creditworthiness.

They also look at factors such as your income, employment history, and outstanding debts, as above. However, being on the voter's list can make the mortgage application process smoother.

To be on the voter's list, you can do this by visiting the gov.uk website, or by contacting your local electoral registration office.

CHAPTER N.3

Income and employment: Lenders will want to see evidence of your income, employment, and any other sources of income you may have.

✳

Income and employment:

INCOME AND EMPLOYMENT: LENDERS WILL WANT TO SEE EVIDENCE OF YOUR INCOME, EMPLOYMENT, AND ANY OTHER SOURCES OF INCOME YOU MAY HAVE.

When applying for a mortgage as a first-time property buyer in the UK, lenders will want to see evidence of your income, employment, and any other sources of income you may have. This is to ensure that you have a stable and reliable source of income to make the monthly mortgage repayments.

One of the most important pieces of information that lenders will require is your employment status. They will want to know if you are currently employed, self-employed, or on a temporary contract, as well as the length of time you have been in your current job. They will also want to see your pay slips and bank statements to verify your income.

If you are self-employed, lenders may require additional documentation, such as your most recent tax returns or business accounts, to verify your income. They will also want to see evidence of your business's stability and profitability.

In addition to your employment income, lenders may also consider other sources of income, such as rental income, dividends, or pensions. If you have multiple sources of income, it can help to demonstrate to the lender that you have a stable and reliable income stream to make the mortgage repayments.

It's also important to consider your outgoings and any other financial commitments you may have when applying for a mortgage.

Lenders will take this into account to assess your affordability and ensure that you have enough disposable income at the end of each month to make the mortgage repayments.

In summary, lenders will want to see evidence of your income, employment, and any other sources of income you may have in order to ensure that you have a stable and reliable source of income to make the mortgage repayments.

It's important to be prepared with the necessary documentation, such as pay slips, bank statements, and tax returns, and to consider your outgoings and other financial commitments when applying for a mortgage.

CHAPTER N.4

Deposit: The larger the deposit you can provide, the better your chances of getting approved for a mortgage and at lower interest rates.

✳

Deposit:

DEPOSIT: THE LARGER THE DEPOSIT YOU CAN PROVIDE, THE BETTER YOUR CHANCES OF GETTING APPROVED FOR A MORTGAGE AND AT LOWER INTEREST RATES.

When applying for a mortgage as a first-time property buyer in the UK, the size of your deposit can have a significant impact on your chances of getting approved and the interest rate you will be offered.

A deposit is the amount of money you put towards the purchase of a property, typically expressed as a percentage of the property's value. The larger the deposit you can provide, the better your chances of getting approved for a mortgage and at a lower interest rate.

The reason for this is that a larger deposit reduces the amount you need to borrow and therefore the risk for the lender.

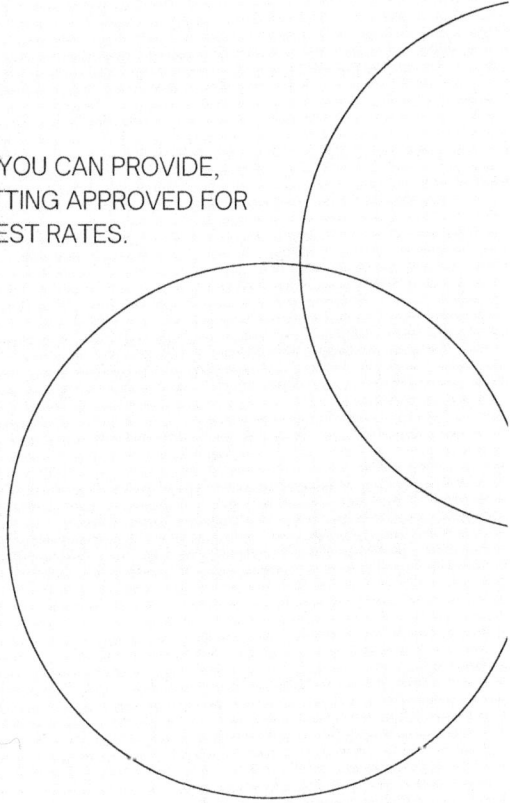

WITH A LARGER DEPOSIT, YOU CAN ALSO ACCESS MORE FAVOURABLE MORTGAGE PRODUCTS, SUCH AS A LOWER INTEREST RATE.

HOW BANKS THINK.

The standard deposit for a first-time buyer mortgage is typically around 5-10% of the property's value; but it can vary depending on the lender and the type of mortgage you are applying for.

Some lenders may require a larger deposit of 15% or more (depending on your credit score), while others may offer mortgages with a smaller deposit.

Regardless, it is important to consider that a larger deposit can also help to reduce the cost of your mortgage over time, as a larger deposit means you will have to borrow less and therefore pay less in interest.

Note however that obtaining a larger deposit can be difficult for first-time buyers, as saving for a deposit can be challenging. There are various government schemes that can help first-time buyers get on the property ladder, such as Help to Buy or Shared Ownership.

Help to Buy, Shared Ownership, Lifetime ISA and Starter Homes: These schemes can help with the deposit and other costs associated with buying a property.

The Help to Buy scheme is a government-backed program that helps first-time buyers and home movers purchase a new-build home with a deposit of as little as 5%. The scheme is available to buyers with a minimum household income of £80,000 (£90,000 in London) and is capped at £600,000 in the UK and £450,000 in London. Under the scheme, buyers can apply for an equity loan of up to 20% of the purchase price (40% in London), interest-free for the first five years.

Another option is the **Shared Ownership scheme.** This scheme is aimed at helping first-time buyers and those on lower incomes to purchase a share of a property, typically between 25% and 75% of the property's value, and pay rent on the remaining share. The scheme is available for properties up to a certain value, which varies depending on the area.

The Lifetime ISA is another government scheme that can help first-time buyers. It is a savings account that allows first-time buyers aged between 18 and 39 to save up to £4,000 per year and receive a 25% bonus from the government on top of their savings, up to a maximum bonus of £1,000 per year. The savings and bonus can be used towards a deposit on a first home.

Finally, the government's **Starter Homes** initiative is a scheme that aims to help first-time buyers purchase new-build homes at a 20% discount.

The initiative is currently being implemented, and the properties will be available to buy from participating house builders and local authorities.

In summary, there are various government schemes available to help first-time buyers in the UK get on the property ladder, such as Help to Buy, Shared Ownership, Lifetime ISA, and Starter Homes. These schemes can help with the deposit and other costs associated with buying a property, and can be a great option for those who may find it difficult to save for a deposit on their own.

The larger the deposit you can provide, the better your chances of getting approved for a mortgage and at a lower interest rate, which can help to reduce the cost of your mortgage over time. As above, obtaining a larger deposit may be difficult for first-time buyers, but there are government schemes available to help.

CHAPTER N.5

How can parents assist first time buyers?

✳

How can parents assist first time buyers?

HOW CAN PARENTS ASSIST FIRST TIME BUYERS?

There are several ways in which parents can assist first-time buyers in purchasing a property. Some of the most common ways include:

1. Financial assistance: Parents can provide financial assistance in the form of a disclosed cash gift, or loan towards the deposit, or help with the cost of legal fees or other expenses associated with purchasing a property.
2. Guarantor: Parents can act as a guarantor on a mortgage, which means they will be responsible for the mortgage payments if the borrower is unable to make them.
3. Joint mortgage: Parents can go on a mortgage with their child, which can increase the amount the child can borrow and make it easier for them to get a mortgage.
4. Rental income: Parents can help their child to build a deposit by renting out a room in their home to them, at a significantly reduced rate, or by renting out a property they own to their child. See 7. below.
5. Help with a down payment: Some parents may choose to help their child with a down payment on a property, this can be especially useful if the child has a low credit score, as it allows them to secure a mortgage with a lower down payment.
6. Co-signing a loan: Some parents may choose to co-sign a loan with their child. This can help the child to secure a mortgage, even if they have limited credit history or a low credit score.
7. Offer to purchase the property: Some parents may choose to purchase the property themselves, rent it out to their child and transfer it to them at a later stage. This can be useful if the child is unable to secure a mortgage on their own.

It's important to note that each option has its own set of risks and benefits, and it's important for both the parents and the first-time buyer to carefully consider the options and the long-term impact of the decision.

It's also worth consulting with a financial advisor or mortgage broker to ensure that the choice is the most appropriate for the specific situation.

In summary, parents can assist first-time buyers in various ways, including providing financial assistance, acting as a guarantor, going on a joint mortgage, renting out a room, helping with a down payment, co-signing a loan, or even purchasing the property themselves.

Each option has its own set of risks and benefits, and it's important to carefully consider the options before making a decision.

LIST OF UK BANKS THAT OFFER GUARANTOR MORTGAGES

There are several UK banks that offer guarantor mortgages, which allow first-time buyers to purchase a property with the help of a guarantor, typically a parent or close relative, who acts as a co-signer on the mortgage. Some of the most well-known banks that offer guarantor mortgages include:

- Aldermore Bank
- Barclays
- Leeds Building Society
- Lloyds Bank
- NatWest
- Post Office Money
- Santander
- TSB
- Virgin Money.

GUARANTOR MORTGAGES

It's important to note that the terms and conditions of guarantor mortgages can vary between banks and lenders, and it's important to research and compare the different options to find the best one for your specific situation. It's also important to be aware of the risks involved and to consult with a financial advisor or mortgage broker to ensure that the choice is the most appropriate for the specific situation.

It's worth mentioning that the above list is not exhaustive and there may be other banks and lenders that offer guarantor mortgages.

Finally, it's always recommended to do your own research and compare the different options before making a decision.

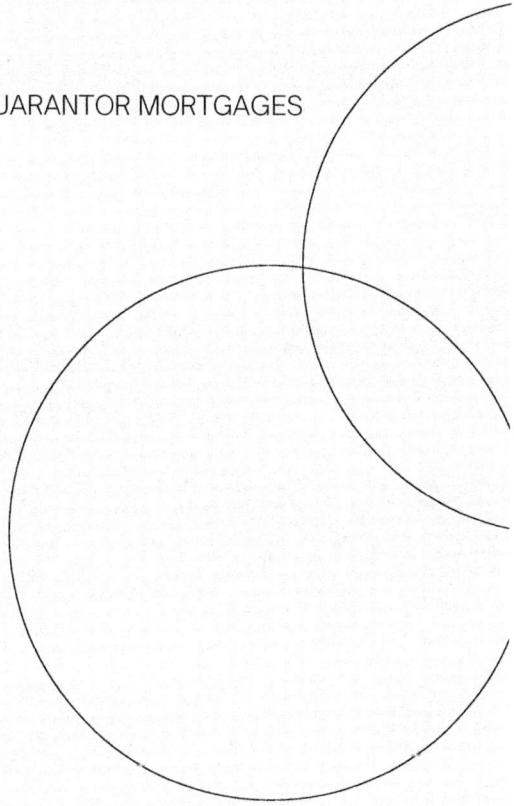

CHAPTER N.6

Bank specialist mortgage brokers & advisors.

*

Bank mortgage brokers & advisors:

BANK SPECIALIST MORTGAGE BROKERS & ADVISORS.

Bank specialist in-house mortgage brokers are mortgage brokers that work for a specific bank or lender. They are responsible for providing mortgage advice and helping customers find the best mortgage products for their specific needs. Some banks and lenders have in-house mortgage brokers that are available to help customers with their mortgage applications.

In-house mortgage brokers typically have access to a wide range of mortgage products offered by the bank or lender they work for, and they can provide customers with expert advice and guidance on the best products for their specific needs. They can also help customers with the application process and answer any questions they may have about the mortgage products offered by the bank or lender.

One of the advantages of using an in-house mortgage broker is that they are able to offer a more personalized service and can provide customers with in-depth knowledge of the bank or lender's products and services. They can also provide customers with exclusive deals and offers that may not be available to non customers.

In-house mortgage brokers, as employees of the bank or lender, will have access to the customer's bank account information as part of the mortgage application process.

This can help the broker to verify the customer's income and financial situation, and to ensure that the customer can afford the mortgage payments.

Having access to the customer's bank account records can also help the mortgage broker to recommend the most suitable mortgage products for the customer.

For example, if the customer has consistent multiple sources of income and a good credit history, the broker may recommend a larger mortgage, at a fixed lower interest rate.

On the other hand, if the customer has a variable income or a less favourable credit history, the broker may recommend a different type of mortgage, and advice, on the best approach, or solution, to achieving a mortgage.

Additionally, access to the customer's weekly/monthly expenditure can help the in-house mortgage broker to provide a more accurate and efficient service. The broker will be able to verify the customer's information more quickly, providing the customer with a decision on the mortgage application promptly.

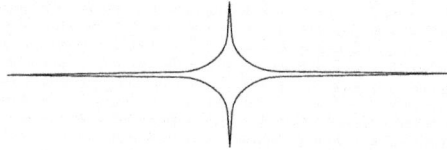

However, it's worth noting that in-house mortgage brokers can only offer products from the bank or lender they work for, and they may not have access to the full range of products available on the market.

In summary, in-house mortgage brokers are mortgage brokers that work for a specific bank or lender and can provide customers with expert advice and guidance on the best mortgage products for their specific needs.

They have access to a wide range of mortgage products offered by the bank or lender they work for and can offer a more personalized service.

However, they may not have access to the full range of products available on the market and may be incentivized to recommend products that are more profitable for the bank or lender.

It is important to note that, depending on the bank, in-house mortgage brokers are usually FREE, compared to external mortgage brokers.

It's important to compare with other options and consult with a financial advisor to ensure that the choice is the most appropriate for the specific situation.

CHAPTER N.7

Affordability:

✳

Affordability.

AFFORDABILITY: LENDERS WILL ASSESS YOUR AFFORDABILITY BY LOOKING AT YOUR INCOME, OUTGOINGS, AND OTHER FINANCIAL COMMITMENTS TO ENSURE YOU CAN AFFORD THE MORTGAGE REPAYMENTS.

When applying for a mortgage as a first-time property buyer in the UK, lenders will assess your affordability to ensure that you can afford the mortgage repayments. Affordability is a measure of your ability to repay a mortgage based on your income, outgoings, and other financial commitments.

When assessing affordability, lenders will look at your income, including your salary, any bonuses, and other sources of income, such as rental income or dividends. They will also consider your outgoings, including your bills, debts, groceries and other expenses, to ensure that you have enough disposable income to make the mortgage repayments.

Lenders will also look at other financial commitments, such as credit card debts, personal loans, and car finance, to ensure that you have enough disposable income to make the mortgage repayments. They will also take into account any other dependents you may have, such as children or elderly relatives, to ensure that you have enough disposable income to support them as well.

The lender will also look at the loan-to-income ratio, which is the ratio of the mortgage amount to the borrower's income. This can help them to determine the borrower's ability to repay the mortgage.

In order to ensure that you can afford the mortgage repayments, it's important to be realistic about your income, outgoings, and other financial commitments.

It's also important to be prepared with the necessary documentation, such as pay slips, bank statements, and bills, to demonstrate your income and weekly/outgoings outgoings to the lender.

When applying for a mortgage, lenders will typically use several methods to assess your affordability, including:

1. Income Verification: Lenders will want to see evidence of your income, such as pay slips and bank statements, to verify your ability to make the mortgage repayments. They will also want to see evidence of your employment, such as a letter from your employer or a contract of employment, to ensure that you have a stable income. Lenders will also want to see a P60 form from your employer.
2. Outgoings and Expenses: Lenders will want to see evidence of your outgoings, such as bills and credit card statements, to ensure that you have enough disposable income to make the mortgage repayments. In addition to this, lenders may want to verify two-to-three years' certified accounts from an accountant if you're self-employed. They will also consider other expenses you may have, such as childcare or travel costs, to ensure that you have enough money to cover these costs as well as the mortgage repayments.
3. Credit Check: As above, lenders will conduct a credit check to assess your creditworthiness and to see if you have any outstanding debts or financial commitments. This will help them to determine if you are able to manage your finances responsibly and if you are likely to keep up with the mortgage repayments.
4. Debt-to-Income Ratio: Lenders will assess your overall debt-to-income ratio, which is the proportion of your income that goes towards paying off your debts. A high debt-to-income ratio can indicate that you may struggle to make the mortgage repayments, so lenders will take this into consideration when assessing your affordability.
5. Affordability Calculators: Lenders will use affordability calculators to assess your affordability, these calculators take into account your income, outgoings, and other financial commitments to determine how much you can afford to borrow.

In summary, to assess your income, outgoings, financial commitments, and affordability, lenders will take into account factors that may affect your ability to afford the mortgage repayments.

One of the most important factors that lenders will consider is your credit score and credit history.

A good credit score and credit history can help to increase your chances of getting approved for a mortgage, while a poor credit score or credit history can make it more difficult to get approved.

Lenders will check your credit score and history to assess your creditworthiness and to determine how likely you are to make the mortgage repayments on time.

Another factor that lenders will consider is your employment status and income stability. Lenders prefer borrowers with a stable income and long-term employment, as they are seen as less risky. Self-employed borrowers may be required to provide additional documentation such as business accounts and tax returns to prove their income.

Lenders will also take into account your current living expenses and other financial commitments, such as credit card debts, loans, and other outgoings. They will assess your overall debt-to-income ratio to ensure that you can afford the mortgage repayments while still being able to manage your other financial commitments.

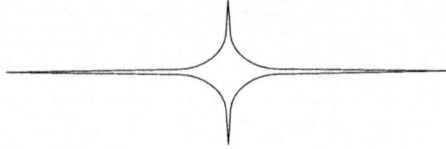

Lenders will also consider the type of property you are buying and its location.

Properties in high-demand areas or those that are considered as low-risk investments may be more likely to be approved than properties in less desirable areas or that are considered as high-risk investments.

It's important to note that lenders have different affordability criteria and some may be more lenient than others. However, it's always important to be honest and transparent about your income, outgoings, and other financial commitments when applying for a mortgage.

Finally, it's important to be aware that the lender's affordability criteria may change over time and to check with the lender before applying for the mortgage.

CHAPTER N.8

Types of mortgages.

*

Types of mortgages.

TYPES OF MORTGAGES: THERE ARE DIFFERENT TYPES OF MORTGAGES AVAILABLE, SUCH AS FIXED RATE, TRACKER, AND VARIABLE RATE, AND YOU SHOULD RESEARCH AND COMPARE THESE TO FIND THE BEST OPTION FOR YOU. THE BEST PLACE TO START IS TO SPEAK WITH YOUR BANK.

When it comes to buying a home, one of the most important decisions you'll make is choosing the right type of mortgage. There are several different options available, each with its own set of pros and cons. We'll take a closer look at three of the most common types of mortgages: fixed rate, tracker, and variable rate.

Fixed rate mortgages are the most popular type of home loan in the UK. They offer the security of knowing that your interest rate will stay the same for the entire duration of the fixed term. This means your monthly payments will be consistent, and you'll be able to budget accordingly. However, fixed rate mortgages may have a higher interest rate than other types of mortgages, so you may end up paying more in interest over the life of the loan.

Tracker mortgages, also known as variable rate mortgages (VRMs), have an interest rate that is tied to a specific index, such as the Bank of England base rate, which it follows during a specified period. The interest rate can fluctuate based on changes to the index, which means your monthly payments could change.

Tracker mortgages typically have a lower interest rate than fixed rate mortgages, but the rate can change over time, making it difficult to budget.

Variable rate mortgages can fluctuate based on a variety of factors such as inflation and market conditions.

The loan term is the length of time you have to pay off the loan. The most common loan terms are 15 and 30 years, but some lenders may also offer 20 or 25-year terms.

A shorter loan term will result in higher monthly payments, but you will pay less in interest over the life of the loan. On the other hand, a longer loan term will result in lower monthly payments, but you will pay more in interest over the life of the loan.

When choosing a mortgage, it's also important to consider the overall terms of the loan. For example, the loan term, down payment, and closing costs can all have an impact on your monthly payments and the overall cost of the loan.

When deciding on the best type of mortgage for you, it's important to consider your financial situation, your budget, and your future plans. If you're comfortable with the idea of your interest rate and monthly payments changing, a tracker or variable rate mortgage may be a good option for you.

On the other hand, if you want the security of a fixed rate and consistent monthly payments, a fixed rate mortgage may be the way to go. It's important to do your research and compare the different types of mortgages to find the one that best suits your needs.

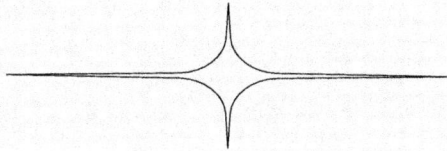

CHAPTER N.9

Fees:

*

Fees:

There may be fees associated with taking out a mortgage, such as arrangement fees and valuation fees, which you should factor into your budget. We'll take a closer look at some of the most common fees associated with mortgages.

When taking out a mortgage, it's important to consider all of the costs associated with the loan. In addition to the interest rate and monthly payments, there may also be various fees that you'll need to pay. These fees can add up quickly and can have a significant impact on the overall cost of the loan.

One of the most common fees associated with mortgages is the arrangement fee. This fee is charged by the lender for setting up the loan and can range from a few hundred to a few thousand pounds. It covers the cost of processing and underwriting the loan, as well as any other administrative costs associated with setting up the loan.

Another common fee is the valuation fee. This fee is charged by the lender to cover the cost of an independent property valuation, which is required to determine the value of the property you're buying.

The fee can vary depending on the size and type of property, but it's typically a few hundred pounds.

It is not unusual for some lenders to charge an application fee, which is a fee for processing your loan application. This fee can range from a few hundred to a few thousand pounds, depending on the lender.

There may also be additional fees that you'll need to pay, such as legal fees, survey fees, and title insurance.

These fees can vary depending on the lender and the specific loan, so it's important to ask about fees when comparing mortgage options, which will help with your planning and budgeting.

When budgeting for a mortgage, it's important to factor in all of the associated fees, not just the interest rate and monthly payments. Be sure to ask your lender and broker for a detailed breakdown of all the fees associated with the loan and compare them with other available market options.

Closing costs are the fees associated with the loan, such as appraisal fees, title fees, and origination fees. These costs can add up quickly, so it's important to factor them into your budget when comparing mortgage options. Some lenders may also offer no-fee mortgages, but they may have higher interest rates to compensate.

When it comes to choosing a mortgage, it's important to consider all of the factors involved and compare the different options available.

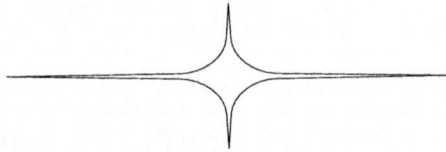

It's a good idea to consult with a mortgage professional or a financial advisor to get a better understanding of the process and to ensure that you make the best decision for your specific situation.

It's also a good idea to shop around and compare fees from different lenders to ensure that you're getting the best deal.

In conclusion, it's important to be aware of the various fees associated with mortgages and factor them into your budget when making a decision.

It's also advisable to shop around, compare fees and interest rates, and consult with a mortgage professional or financial advisor to ensure that you make the best decision for your specific situation.

CHAPTER N.10

Legal fees:

✳

Legal fees:

You will need to pay for a solicitor to handle the legal side of buying a property. We'll take a closer look at legal fees and what you can expect to pay when buying a property.

When buying a property, there are a number of costs that you'll need to consider, one of which is legal fees. These fees are typically associated with hiring a solicitor, or a conveyancer, to handle the legal side of the transaction. The cost of legal fees can vary depending on the type of property, the location, and the complexity of the transaction.

Instructing a solicitor, or a conveyancer, is one of the important steps towards home ownership. This will typically involve a number of tasks such as:

- Reviewing the contract and any land supporting documents.
- Carrying out local authority and environmental searches.
- Reviewing and advising on the lease (if applicable).
- Obtaining and reviewing the title deeds.
- Dealing with the Land Registry [including registration following a purchase].
- Exchange of contracts.
- Handling the transfer of funds, and importantly, the completion of the sale.

The cost of legal fees will vary depending on the solicitor or conveyancer you choose. Some firms may charge a fixed fee, while others may charge an hourly rate.

The cost can range from a few hundred pounds to several thousand pounds, depending on the complexity of the transaction.

It's important to note that legal fees are not the only costs associated with buying a property. You'll also need to pay for other expenses such as stamp duty, land registry fees, and 'disbursements'.

'Disbursements' are costs incurred by the solicitor on your behalf, such as the cost of obtaining a mortgage valuation, telegraphic transfer fees or 'local authority search' fees.

When budgeting for a property, it's important to factor in all of the costs associated with the purchase, including legal fees. Be sure to ask your solicitor or conveyancer for a detailed breakdown of all the costs associated with the transaction, and compare them with other options.

It's also a good idea to shop around and compare fees from different solicitors or conveyancers to ensure that you're getting the best deal.

The Law Society of England and Wales provides a free referral service for anyone looking for legal services. Going to the Law Society for a solicitor, or a conveyancer, can have a number of benefits, including:

1. Professionalism: The Law Society is a professional body that sets standards for solicitors and conveyancers. By choosing a solicitor or conveyancer that is registered with the Law Society, you can be confident that they have the necessary qualifications and experience to handle your legal matter.
2. Protection: The Law Society has a complaints and disciplinary procedure in place to protect consumers. If you are not satisfied with the service provided by a solicitor or conveyancer that is registered with the Law Society, you can make a complaint and have it investigated.
3. Expertise: The Law Society has a wide range of expertise and resources available to its members, which can be beneficial when handling legal matters. This includes access to up-to-date information on legislation and case law, as well as training and development opportunities.
4. Professional Indemnity Insurance: The Law society also ensures that its members have professional indemnity insurance, which can provide protection for clients if something goes wrong.
5. Trust: The Law Society is a well-established and reputable organization, and choosing a solicitor or conveyancer that is registered with it can give you peace of mind that you are working with a professional who is held to a high standard.

It's always important to check if the solicitor or conveyancer you are planning to use is registered with the Law society, and also check their reviews, feedback and reputation.

In conclusion, legal fees are an important cost to consider when buying a property. It's essential to budget for them and to shop around to ensure you are getting the best deal.

Be sure to ask your solicitor or conveyancer for a detailed breakdown of all the costs associated with the transaction, including a 'Completion Statement' which should be provided at the end of the purchase, and always compare the fees to other options available.

CHAPTER N.11

The problem of short leaseholds.

*

The problem of short leaseholds.

THE PROBLEM OF SHORT LEASEHOLDS.

The risks associated with short leaseholds is a point most property buyers ignore, and this is not limited to first-time buyers alone.

Short term leases usually occur when the owner/leaseholder does not extend their lease, or the lease is below 70 years.

The significant risk associated with a short lease, is that it is much harder to sell. As the lease on a property reduces year-over-year, the more it's value declines. This makes the property unappealing for prospective buyers, as well as for mortgage lenders. Most banks will not provide mortgages for properties with short leases, particularly in a difficult market, and it is usually expensive to extend the lease.

Expired leasehold properties, or flats will usually revert to a freehold property and come under the ownership of the freeholder.

This implies that you no longer have tenancy and the freeholder is able to regain full possession of the property.

For first-time buyers, at the outset [during your property search], it is important to seek properties with leases between 125 years and 999 years, including and preferably a 'Share of the Freehold'.

Additionally, you must factor in the cost of any service charges, ground rent and maintenance fees within the terms of the lease, which may add significant costs to the overall ownership of the property.

In some cases, the leasehold terms may also include restrictions on what the owner can do with the property, such as making certain renovations or subletting.

This can make it difficult for the owner to make use of the property in the way that they would like.

Seek professional or legal advice before you commence the legal/buying process, to avoid needless cost, and to ensure that you make the best decision for your specific situation.

CHAPTER N.12

Why it is important to undertake a home inspection, independent property valuation and home appraisal before buying a property as a first-time buyer.

✳

Why it is important to undertake a home inspection, independent property valuation and home appraisal before buying a property as a first-time buyer.

WHY IT IS IMPORTANT TO UNDERTAKE A HOME INSPECTION, INDEPENDENT PROPERTY VALUATION AND HOME APPRAISAL BEFORE BUYING A PROPERTY AS A FIRST-TIME BUYER.

A home inspection is important because it can do the following - reveal any potential issues or problems with the property that may not be immediately obvious to the buyer; identify areas where major repairs or renovations require immediate attention, and, identify any work that needs to be completed in the future.

Having a home inspection can help a buyer make an informed decision about whether to purchase the property, or if they need to negotiate with the seller to make repairs or address potential issues.

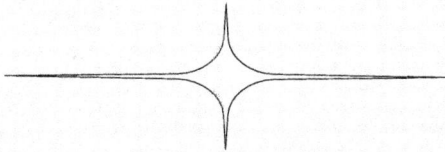

A home appraisal is important because it provides an independent, professional assessment of the value of the property.

This can help the buyer determine if they are paying a fair price for the property and can also be used to secure financing for the purchase.

Additionally, it helps in determining the value of the property in case of any disputes regarding property value.

Both the home inspection, valuation and appraisal are important steps in the process of buying a property, especially for first-time buyers who may not have experience with the process or knowledge of what to look for when purchasing a home.

CHAPTER N.13

Insurance: Why buildings and contents insurance are important.

✳

Insurance: Why buildings and contents insurance are important.

INSURANCE: WHY BUILDINGS AND CONTENTS INSURANCE ARE IMPORTANT.

When buying a new home, it's important to think about insurance to protect your investment. Buildings and contents insurance are two types of insurance that are particularly important to consider.

Buildings insurance is a type of insurance that covers the structure of your home, including the walls, roof, and any permanent fixtures and fittings. This type of insurance is usually required by mortgage lenders as a condition of the loan. It protects you against damage caused by events such as fire, storm, flood, and theft. It also covers the cost of any repairs or rebuilding that may be needed in the event of damage.

Contents insurance, on the other hand, covers your personal possessions inside the home, such as furniture, appliances, and clothing. This type of insurance is not usually required by mortgage lenders, but it is still important to have as it will protect your personal possessions in case of loss or damage. It also covers you for events like theft, fire, and flooding.

When taking out buildings and contents insurance, it's important to consider the level of coverage you need. You may need to purchase extra coverage for high-value items such as jewelry, artwork, or antiques. It's also important to consider the location of your home and the risks associated with that area, such as flooding or wildfire.

It's also important to review your insurance policies regularly, and update it as your needs change.

For example, if you make any major renovations, you may need to update your buildings insurance coverage. Additionally, if you acquire new valuable items, you may need to increase your contents insurance coverage.

When shopping for insurance, it is important to compare different policies and coverage options to find the one that best suits your needs. Don't hesitate to ask for help. An insurance broker or financial advisor can help you to find the best coverage for your needs.

In conclusion, buildings and contents insurance are important types of insurance to consider when buying a new home. They will protect your investment and your personal possessions in case of loss or damage. It's important to consider the level of coverage you need, and to review your insurance policies regularly to ensure that they continue to meet your needs.

Additional Tips & Conclusion:

ADDITIONAL TIPS:

Do A Final Walkthrough: Research your chosen area.

It is important to do a final walkthrough around the property, the streets and community to understand the environment and neighbourhood, access to schools, bus links, train stations and facilities, as well as your potential neighbours, to ensure the purchase will be a perfect fit before moving forward with the purchase and taking ownership of the property.

It is also important to check the crime rate of an area before buying a property, because this can provide insights into the overall safety and security of the area.

High crime rates can be a red flag for potential buyers, and insurance companies, and can affect the overall value and desirability of a property.

In the United Kingdom, you can research trends within a neighbourhood, including crime rates, by visiting the website of the local police force or by using online tools like crime maps or crime statistics websites.

These tools can provide information on the types of crime that have occurred in the area, as well as the frequency of those crimes. Additionally, you can check with the local neighbourhood watch groups to get an idea of their experience in the area.

Specific tools include, **ADT, Check My Street, Crime Statistics, Our Watch, Crime Rate, In Your Area**, e.t.c

Finally, it is important to research removal companies.

If you don't own a lot of furniture to move into your new home, you could hire a removal van yourself, or speak to family and friends.

However, if you do own a tonne of household furniture it may be advisable to instruct a removal company.

Costs will depend on the number of items you intend to move and the distance to your new property.

<u>Once again, seek professional advice on every step of the transaction process.</u>

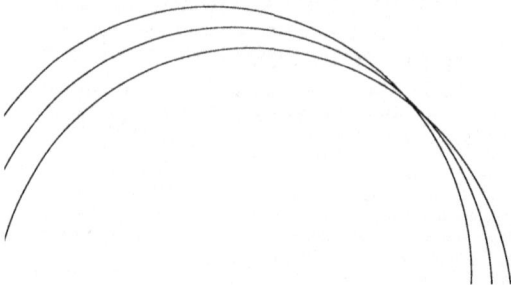

Printed in Great Britain
by Amazon

39168228R10030